Vote for Laughter
Book of Political Cartoons

Featuring Cartoons From
Air Mail
Barron's
The New Yorker
and more!

Front Cover illustration: J. B. Handelsman
Back Cover illustration: Bob Mankoff
Introduction: Bob Mankoff
Editor: Darren Kornblut

Cartoon Collections, LLC
10 Grand Central, 29th Floor
New York, NY 10017

For cartoon licensing information visit www.cartoonstock.com
Create a personalized version of this book at www.cartoonstockgifts.com

First edition published 2024

Item # 47625
ISBN: 978-1-963079-14-2

Introduction

Welcome to a world where wit meets governance, and satire sharpens its teeth on the bones of political follies. As the former cartoon editor of *The New Yorker*, I've always cherished how cartoons cut through the clutter of political discourse, delivering insights with a punchline. In this collection, we present the crème de la crème of political cartoons, a convergence of art and attitude that captures the spirit of our times with a smirk and a raised eyebrow.

These cartoons are more than mere sketches; they are weapons of mass discussion, igniting debates and laughter in equal measure. They hold a mirror up to our leaders, reflecting the absurdities that might otherwise escape unscathed in the somber drone of everyday news. Here, no policy is too ponderous, no political position too dignified to escape the cartoonist's incisive pen.

As you flip through these pages, expect to chuckle, cringe, and perhaps even shout in agreement or dismay. Each cartoon is a story—a compact, yet powerful narrative that challenges the status quo, questions the power structures, and delivers a dose of healthy skepticism, all while entertaining you.

So, sit back, relax, and let the power of cartoons refresh your perspective, proving that sometimes, the truth is funnier than fiction.

"O.K., the third of July is out. How about the fourth?"

"The majority of voters have disapproved of the way you handled the former environment."

"Do you have another form of photo I.D.?"

5

"When it comes to legislation, I will not be intimidated by pressure from the American People."

"I'm leaving politics to spend more
time with my legal defense team."

"*Place your left hand on the Bible, raise your right hand, and repeat after me, 'Wow, I can't believe this is happening to me.'*"

"Use diplomacy. If that fails, you could try force."

"Perhaps we should provide for the separation of state and entertainment."

"It always amazes me how extremely simple creatures, with no capacity for communication, can achieve the appearance of joint decision-making."

"*Still, you've got to applaud the transparency.*"

"*Major Funding. How much do you need?*"

"Take us to literally anyone but your leader."

"Remember, my cover story is that
I'm leaving politics to spend time with you."

"The peasants are mercilessly ridiculing you online."

"*Does it trouble you that he's started putting the word 'constitution' in air quotes?*"

"Just this once, can we not talk about news or politics or money or family
or relationships or children or friends or sex or religion or sports
or culture or real estate or the past or the future?"

"I know it's just a political buzzword, but the
idea of change really resonates with me."

"My fellow-candidates..."

"I can do whatever I want—I come from a safe district."

"Look, I know I'm here to answer some tough questions,
but could I have some easy ones to warm up with?"

"I may be awhile. I'm soliciting funds for my reelection campaign."

"If elected, I'll institute an *AMAZING CRASH PROGRAM* that in *JUST 24 HOURS* will trim fat and waste from government and literally turn it into *SUPER SERVICES* for you the *AMERICAN PEOPLE* by utilizing a *NATURAL MECHANISM* so powerful that when unleashed against pokcets of government flab it melts and transforms them into effective programs that work even as the American people sleep!"

"All I did was remove his flag pin!"

"Let's face it—I'm a bit of a control freak."

"But how do you know for sure you've got power unless you abuse it?"

"You know, the idea of taxation *with* representation doesn't appeal to me very *much*, either."

"Founding Fathers! How come no Founding Mothers?"

"*With an average vote of 3.5 stars,*
the legislation is passed."

"*May we live in interesting times. And may we outlive them.*"

"Hey! There's no soap in here."

"His vote doesn't count, but at least he gets a
sense of being part of the process."

"Makes me want to draw up some districts of my own."

"Other countries are laughing at us!"

"I'll vote for anyone who isn't a dog."

"I consider myself bipartisan-curious."

"Diane, haven't we anyone at
the state department who talks turkey?"

"*Not only must I succeed, ... others must also pay my taxes.*"

ALL RHETORIC ABANDON,
YE WHO ENTER HERE!

MEDIA HELL

"He tells it like it is."

"Vote for me and the baby lives."

"Let me answer your question by saying that you're being really
aggressive, and it's totally freaking me out."

"Of course, we'd make better time if we weren't towing the press barge."

"*But what if a tyrant comes to power and no one's able to stop him because the whole thing's kind of funny.*"

"Sh-h-h. It's a birthday card for Liechtenstein. Sign it and pass it on."

"And I like the fact that all amounts are given in 'illions'
—it gives us room to maneuver."

"Daddy's going of to defeat terrorism in subtler, economic ways."

"I have a brief statement, a clarification, and two denials."

"*Martha, are you sure you're not marrying me for money?*"

"Good evening, and welcome to
the Situation Room."

"The President wants a calm, measured, evenhanded speech that kicks some serious butt."

"Now for yout stress test."

"*Are you sure everyone will know we're being ironic?*"

"*With great ignorance comes great confidence.*"

"O.K., who else is writing a book?"

"I'm not running for reelection. I already have enough material for my book."

"I don't mind out of control spending as long as it's on stuff I like."

"You know what I like about power? It's so damn empowering."

"I'm back. My family didn't want to spend more time with me."

ON THE CAMPAIGN TRAIL

"I'll find you some candy, but first tell me how you got past the Secret Service."

"Politics has divided everything."

"Can't we put in something about rich
white guys don't have to pay taxes?"

"I'm afraid my youthful transgressions may already have eliminated any chance for me to be President."

"Who told the press we were having a bad hair day?"

"Gentlemen, it's time we gave some serious thought to the effects of global warming."

SENATORS ARE ALLOWED TWO FROM EACH STATE.

"That's an excellent prescreened question, but before I give you my stock answer I'd like to try to disarm everyone with a carefully rehearsed joke."

"I don't think you can distance yourself from the White House on this one. After all, you are the President."

"I'm undecided, but that doesn't mean I'm apathetic or uninformed."

"Relax, Mr. President, that's not a migrant caravan.
It's just the city marathon."

"If we don't comply, they're threatening us with liberation."

"The only solution I can see is to hold a series of long and costly hearings in order to put off finding a solution."

"I appreciate the new campaign finance laws, but I miss the thrill of getting around the old ones."

LINCOLN GOES GOTH, WHILE WASHINGTON FAVORS ROCKABILLY, AND HAMILTON REMAINS MOSTLY MOZART.

"I guess we'll all just have to vote a little bit harder next time."

"What I'd like is different presidential candidates, but
I guess I'll just have the shrimp in garlic sauce."

"And no more sex scandals!"

"Don't think of them as terrorist states. Think of them as terrorist markets."

"Neither party seems to be talking about cats."

"*Fiscally yours....*"

PLEASE ENJOY THIS CULTURALLY, ETHNICALLY, RELIGIOUSLY, AND POLITICALLY CORRECT CARTOON RESPONSIBLY. THANK YOU.

SHAW

Index of Artists

www.ingramcontent.com/pod-product-compliance
Lightning Source LLC
Chambersburg PA
CBHW040848100426

42813CB00015B/2744